Text copyright © 2008 by Mona Kerby
Pictures copyright © 2008 by Lynne Barasch
All rights reserved
Distributed in Canada by Douglas & McIntyre Ltd.
Color separations by Embassy Graphics
Printed and bound in China by South China Printing Co. Ltd.
Designed by Nancy Goldenberg
First edition, 2008
1 3 5 7 9 10 8 6 4 2

www.fsgkidsbooks.com

Library of Congress Cataloging-in-Publication Data
Kerby, Mona.
   Owney, the mail pouch pooch / Mona Kerby ; pictures by Lynne Barasch.— 1st ed.
     p.   cm.
   Summary: In 1888, Owney, a stray terrier puppy, finds a home in the Albany, New York,
post office and becomes its official mascot as he rides the mail train through the Adirondacks
and beyond, criss-crossing the United States, into Canada and Mexico, and eventually
traveling around the world by mail boat in 132 days.
   ISBN-13: 978-0-374-35685-9
   ISBN-10: 0-374-35685-8
   1. Owney (Dog)—Juvenile fiction.   [1. Owney (Dog)—Fiction.   2. Terriers—Fiction.
3. Dogs—Fiction.   4. Mascots—Fiction.   5. Postal service—Fiction.   6. Voyages and
Travels—Fiction.]   I. Barasch, Lynne, ill.   II. Title.

PZ10.3.K4845 Own 2008
[Fic]—dc22

                                                                         2006047605

With thanks to Eunice Chang for providing the Chinese characters

OWNEY
THE MAIL-POUCH POOCH

MONA KERBY

PICTURES BY LYNNE BARASCH

Frances Foster Books   Farrar, Straus and Giroux   New York

In memory of our dog, Sam, and to all good dogs everywhere
—M.K.

In memory of Rags, the ultimate dog's dog
—L.B.

In the year 1888, on a cold rainy October night in Albany, New York, a straggly terrier mutt wandered through the empty streets looking for a place to get out of the rain. He was so skinny his ribs stuck out.

At the post office, the back door was opened a crack, and the dog squeezed inside. The room was warm and dry.

He came to a pile of canvas bags. He sniffed around until he found just the right spot, where he circled twice, curled up, and went to sleep.

The next morning, workers found the mutt on the mail pouches. He gave a mean, low-pitched rumble.

The men talked to the dog and asked him his name. The mutt glared. He sniffed. But he didn't bite. He seemed to like the smell of their blue wool uniforms.

Days passed. The dog didn't leave and no one came looking for him, so the men cleaned him up and gave him a name. They called him Owney.

Owney settled in at the Albany Post Office. He patrolled the mail room, nosing out trouble. Rats and cats didn't stand a chance. He supervised the men as they sorted and bagged letters.

Different men took Owney home,
thinking that he might want a family.

But Owney wasn't interested. Each time, he made his way back to the
post office—and to his mail pouches.

In the afternoons, when the men loaded the outgoing mail on the wagon,
Owney stood guard. Then he hopped aboard for the ride to the train depot.
With his ears up and his nose to the wind, he was alert to any danger.

Once when the men returned to the post office with the incoming mail, they discovered they were missing a mail pouch. What's more, Owney was missing, too.

One man headed back to the train depot. He found the missing mail pouch. Owney was sitting on top of it. But when the man tried to get the bag, Owney growled. He showed his teeth and refused to give it up. The worker was out of uniform, and Owney was not about to turn over government property to just anybody.

The man raced back to the office, where he grabbed a canvas bag and located a friend in uniform. Together they went back to the depot and found Owney, still guarding the U.S. Mail.

The men walked slowly up to Owney. He sniffed the bag. He sniffed the legs of the blue wool uniform. He lowered his ears, wagged his tail, and hopped off the pouch.

After that, his pals bought him an official-looking collar with a tag that read: "Owney, Post Office, Albany, New York."

A few weeks later at the depot, as the train started pulling away, Owney chased after it. Running lickety-split, he leaped and landed in the mail car.

The Albany men were sad.

The train crew waved their hats. They were glad to have Owney aboard.

All the way to New York City, Owney sat in the open doorway, seeing new sights and sniffing new smells.

The Albany postmen looked for Owney on the next train from New York—and the next, and the train after that. Days and weeks went by, but Owney didn't return.

Several months later, the Albany postmen were at the train depot when, lo and behold, Owney jumped off the mail train.

His friends asked him where he had been, but Owney just wagged his tail.

After that, the men tied a note to his collar. "Dear Railway Postmen: Owney guards the U.S. Mail. Will you let us know where he has been? Please attach your depot tag to his collar."

It wasn't long before Owney hopped another train.

The next time Owney showed up in Albany, he had so many tags hanging from his collar that he could barely lift his head. The postal employees tried to remove some to make his load a little lighter. But Owney didn't like that. He growled.

So his pals bought a harness that stretched across his back and around his chest. They spread his silver and brass medals all over his body instead of under his neck. This made it easier for Owney to walk. He liked it fine.

Owney took off again, crisscrossing the country on the mail trains. He
visited New York City, Brooklyn, Boston, and Augusta, Maine. He saw
Cleveland, Cincinnati, and Fort Wayne. He traveled to Chicago, St. Paul,
Duluth, the Dakota Territory, Seattle, San Francisco, and Los Angeles.
In Texas, he inspected Fort Worth, Waco, San Antonio, Houston, and
Galveston. He hopped a train to Denver, Kansas City, Omaha, Memphis,
New Orleans, Key West, Washington, D.C., and Baltimore. And Owney
stopped at all the small towns in between. Some say he even inspected the
trains and depots in Alaska, Canada, and Mexico.

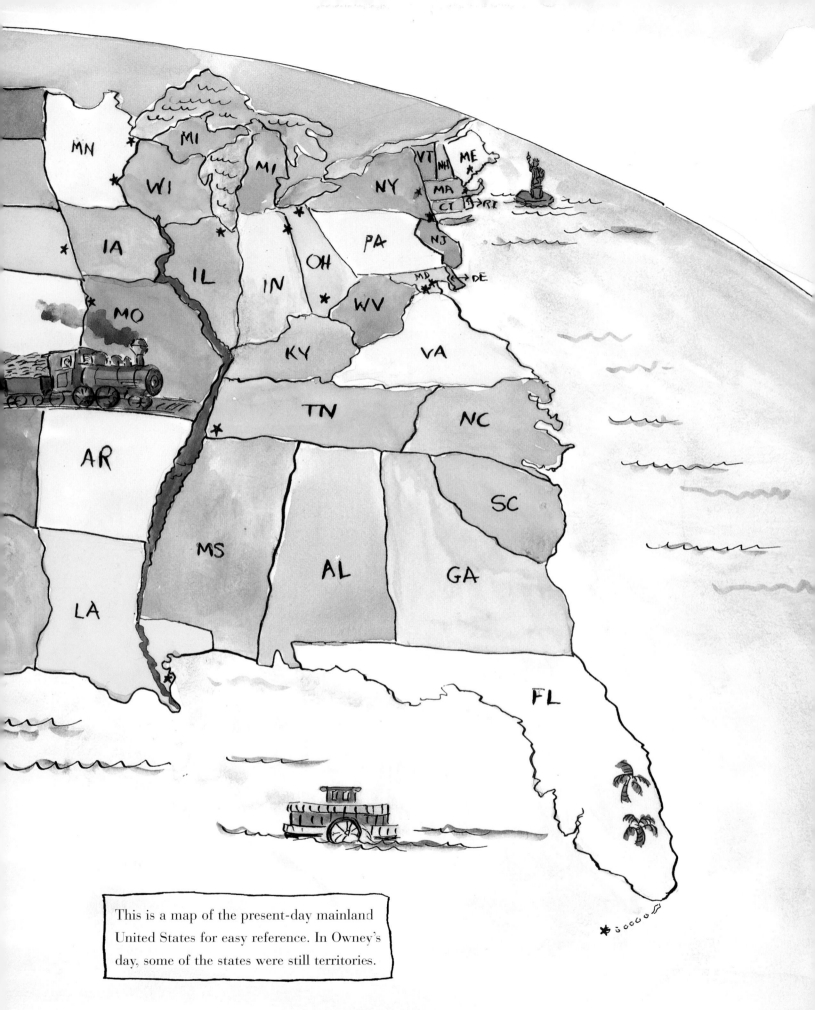

This is a map of the present-day mainland United States for easy reference. In Owney's day, some of the states were still territories.

Owney guarded the mail and the men in their blue wool uniforms. If a railway man fell asleep when it was time to pitch out or pick up a pouch, Owney barked him awake.

In those days, there were lots of train wrecks. But no train ever had an accident when Owney was onboard. Railroad crews called him a good-luck dog.

Owney not only picked up tags from the railway postmen, he also collected trinkets and coupons. Some read: "To his dogship," "Owney, call again," "Good for 25 cents in furniture at S. A. Rathbun's dry goods, Pontiac, Illinois," "One quart of milk at Nashville, Tennessee," "Good for one drink or cigar from H.J. Thyts of Reno, Nevada."

Owney didn't smoke cigars. He just wanted the trinket. He loved the jingling sound of his medals when he walked.

Not everyone welcomed Owney. In Montreal, Canada, the dogcatchers threw him in the pound. Then they wrote to the postal employees in Albany and demanded two dollars and fifty cents.

Owney's pals paid the fine, and Owney was put on the next train home.

No dog worked harder for the U.S. Postal Service. In 1892, Owney greeted the Republicans at their convention in Buffalo, New York.

In 1893, he met with the Iowa bankers in Council Bluffs, Iowa.

In 1895, he welcomed the chicken farmers at the Tacoma, Washington, Poultry Association.

But Owney was beginning to slow down. He was at least eight years old, which is old for a dog, especially one that has spent a lifetime jumping on and off trains. His friends decided to give him a trip around the world, by mail boat. He had his own suitcase with a blanket, comb, and brush.

Before Owney could travel, his pals had to make up a new mailing rate. They called it "Registered Dog Package." And they attached this note to his harness:

To all who may meet this dog: Owney is his name. He is the pet of 100,000 postal employees of the United States of America . . . Treat him kindly.

On August 19, 1895, Owney boarded the steamship *Victoria* in Tacoma, Washington.

Since the mail was in no danger of falling off the boat, Owney didn't have
to spend all his time supervising. He chased rats. And in the afternoons, he
curled up on a mail pouch. In a way, he was still doing his job.

When the ship arrived in Japan, the customs officials didn't know what to do with a traveling dog. They issued Owney an imperial passport—with restrictions. He was not allowed to ride a horse to a fire. He could not rent a house. He could not scribble on buildings. Owney obeyed—after all, he was a U.S. Postal Employee.

From Japan, Owney went to China and then on to Hong Kong. While his shipboard pals rode in rickshaws, Owney followed behind, keeping an eye on everything.

He sailed up the Suez Canal, but he didn't get to stay long enough in Egypt to see the pyramids. He sailed into the harbor of Algiers on the Mediterranean Sea and then to São Miguel in the Azores Islands in the Atlantic Ocean.

And, finally, he arrived in New York City.

Owney finished his world trip in his favorite way—by train. On December 29, 1895, he arrived back in Tacoma, Washington. His trip lasted 132 days. He wore two hundred new tags, trinkets, and ribbons. He had gained six pounds.

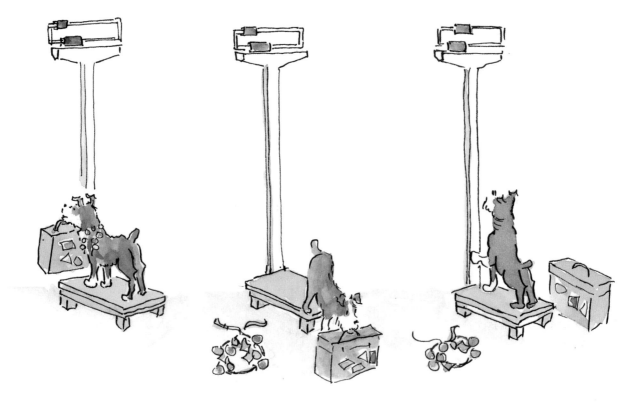

In 1896, at the San Francisco dog show, surrounded by fancy-looking dogs and their fancy-dressed owners, two postal employees stood at attention. One wore a blue wool uniform, the other his natural fur. The judge presented Owney with a medal—"Greatest Dog Traveler in the World."

In the spring of 1897, when the National Association of Railway Clerks invited Owney to their convention in San Francisco, he took one last trip. By now, he was missing some teeth and blind in one eye. Stiff-legged, he could no longer catch a moving train.

In the huge auditorium, the curtains opened. Owney walked to the center of the stage. He was slow, but he still jingled with every step, and his shiny tags sparkled in the spotlight. The crowd leaped to their feet, roaring. For fifteen minutes, they cheered, clapped, and whistled.

After that, there was only one thing to do. Owney had to retire. His pals
sent him home to the Albany Post Office, where his career as a mail dog had
begun. He was given plenty to eat and a soft mail pouch where he could curl
up and fall asleep.

Sometimes on those long, sleepy afternoons, his nose twitched and his
paws quivered. Maybe Owney was dreaming about the good old days—of
running lickety-split to catch a train and traveling the world.

Owney was a great dog. Here he is at work, looking responsible and fierce as he guards four railway men and the mail. He was so famous that most of the major newspapers in the 1890s reported on his travels.

AUTHOR'S NOTE

When Owney died in 1897, his friends had a taxidermist preserve him and sent his body to the Smithsonian Institution in Washington, D.C. I visited him in the Smithsonian's National Postal Museum. At the front door, there's also a bronze statue of Owney with a sign that says to rub him for luck. I did, and I made a wish—that you would enjoy this book. If you visit the museum and rub the statue someday, know that our fingerprints have crossed paths.

To write this story, I began by reading the books written by the staff of the National Postal Museum and examining Owney's file at the National Archives in Washington, D.C. I talked to the city historian of Albany, New York. And I e-mailed many, many librarians who helped me locate newspaper articles.

Whenever possible, I tried to find multiple sources for the same facts. But I found discrepancies in the sources. Since there were several versions of how Owney came to be named, I stated his name and left it at that. One trouble spot was the story about Owney riding the wagons from the post office to the train depot. The Postal Museum cites this story, but the Albany city historian says that in those days, the train tracks ran right behind the post office so the mail could be loaded directly onto the train.

Maybe Owney rode a wagon in another town. Or maybe he didn't. What we do know is this: he loved men who wore blue wool uniforms and he loved the smell of canvas mail pouches.

Thanks to the following people for their help: Virginia Bowers, city historian of Albany, New York; Ellen Gamache at the Albany Public Library; Jody Gripp at the Tacoma Public Library in Washington State; Abigail W. Cooley at the Enoch Pratt Library in Baltimore, Maryland; Lori Holechek at the Carroll County Public Library in Maryland; Sally Jones at Hoover Library at McDaniel College in Westminster, Maryland; Scott Feiner at the Wisconsin Historical Society; Aloha South at the National Archives and Records Administration; and Nancy Pope and Jim O'Donnell at the National Postal Museum.

Owney, proudly posing with his medals

BIBLIOGRAPHY

Bruns, James H. *Mail on the Move*. Polo, Illinois: Transportation Trails, 1992.

"Called to Order: Railway Mail Clerks' Convention Opened." *Los Angeles Times*, March 17, 1897. ProQuest Historical Newspapers database.

Dennis, Wm. J. *The Railway Mail Service*, published in 1916 and located in Owney's file at the National Archives.

"The Largest Cargo of Silk at Tacoma." *The New York Times*, October 27, 1895. From *The Tacoma (Wash.) Ledger*, October 21, 1895. ProQuest Historical Newspapers database.

"Owney a Great Traveler." *The New York Times*, December 24, 1895. ProQuest Historical Newspapers database.

"Owney Sails for Hong Kong." *The Washington Post*, August 20, 1895. ProQuest Historical Newspapers database.

"Owney: The Mascot of the Railway Mail Service." *Los Angeles Times*, March 15, 1896. ProQuest Historical Newspapers database.

"Owney, the Postal Dog." *The Washington Post*, May 2, 1895. ProQuest Historical Newspapers database.

"Owney, the Postoffice Dog." *Los Angeles Times*, December 15, 1895. ProQuest Historical Newspapers database.